FILM FAVORITES

Solos and Band Arrangements
Correlated with Essential Elements® Band Method

Arranged by
MICHAEL SWEENEY, JOHN MOSS and PAUL LAVENDER

Welcome to ESSENTIAL ELEMENTS FILM FAVORITES! The arrangements in this versatile book can be used either in a full concert band setting or as solos for individual instruments. The SOLO pages appear at the beginning of the book, followed by the BAND ARRANGEMENT pages. The supplemental CD recording or PIANO ACCOMPANIMENT book may be used as an accompaniment for solo performance.

ISBN 978-0-634-08692-2

HAL•LEONARD®
CORPORATION
7777 W. BLUEMOUND RD. P.O. BOX 13819 MILWAUKEE, WI 53213

00860144

PIRATES OF THE CARIBBEAN
(A medley including: The Medallion Calls • The Black Pearl)

Eb ALTO CLARINET
Solo

Music by KLAUS BADELT
Arranged by MICHAEL SWEENEY

00860144

From the Paramount and Twentieth Century Fox Motion Picture TITANIC

MY HEART WILL GO ON

(Love Theme From 'Titanic')

Eb ALTO CLARINET
SOLO

Music by JAMES HORNER
Lyric by WILL JENNINGS
Arranged by JOHN MOSS

Andante

00860144

From THE MUPPET MOVIE

THE RAINBOW CONNECTION

Eb ALTO CLARINET
SOLO

Words and Music by
PAUL WILLIAMS and **KENNETH L. ASCHER**
Arranged by PAUL LAVENDER

00860144

From THE LORD OF THE RINGS: THE FELLOWSHIP OF THE RING

MAY IT BE

Eb ALTO CLARINET
Solo

**Words and Music by EITHNE NI BHRAONAIN,
NICKY RYAN and ROMA RYAN**
Arranged by JOHN MOSS

Slowly with emotion

From Walt Disney Pictures' TARZAN™

YOU'LL BE IN MY HEART

Eb ALTO CLARINET
Solo

Words and Music by
PHIL COLLINS
Arranged by MICHAEL SWEENEY

00860144

From the Motion Picture SHREK 2

ACCIDENTALLY IN LOVE

E♭ **ALTO CLARINET**
Solo

Words and Music by
ADAM F. DURITZ
Arranged by MICHAEL SWEENEY

Moderate Rock

Featured in the Motion Picture 2001: A SPACE ODYSSEY

E♭ ALTO CLARINET
Solo

By RICHARD STRAUSS
Arranged by MICHAEL SWEENEY

00860144

From the Paramount Motion Picture MISSION: IMPOSSIBLE

MISSION: IMPOSSIBLE THEME

Eᵇ **ALTO CLARINET**
Solo

By LALO SCHIFRIN
Arranged by MICHAEL SWEENEY

Moderately Fast

MUSIC FROM SHREK

(A medley including: Fairytale Opening • Ride The Dragon)

E♭ ALTO CLARINET
SOLO

Music by JOHN POWELL
and HARRY GREGSON-WILLIAMS
Arranged by JOHN MOSS

From the TriStar Motion Picture THE MASK OF ZORRO
ZORRO'S THEME

E♭ **ALTO CLARINET**
Solo

Composed by
JAMES HORNER
Arranged by JOHN MOSS

PIRATES OF THE CARIBBEAN

(A medley including: The Medallion Calls • The Black Pearl)

E♭ **ALTO CLARINET**
Band Arrangement

Music by KLAUS BADELT
Arranged by MICHAEL SWEENEY

From the Paramount and Twentieth Century Fox Motion Picture TITANIC

MY HEART WILL GO ON

(Love Theme From 'Titanic')

Eb ALTO CLARINET
Band Arrangement

Music by JAMES HORNER
Lyric by WILL JENNINGS
Arranged by JOHN MOSS

THE RAINBOW CONNECTION

Eb ALTO CLARINET
Band Arrangement

Words and Music by
PAUL WILLIAMS and **KENNETH L. ASCHER**
Arranged by PAUL LAVENDER

00860144

From THE LORD OF THE RINGS: THE FELLOWSHIP OF THE RING

MAY IT BE

Eb ALTO CLARINET
Band Arrangement

Words and Music by EITHNE NI BHRAONAIN,
NICKY RYAN and ROMA RYAN
Arranged by JOHN MOSS

From Walt Disney Pictures' TARZAN™
YOU'LL BE IN MY HEART

Eb ALTO CLARINET
Band Arrangement

**Words and Music by
PHIL COLLINS**
Arranged by MICHAEL SWEENEY

From the Motion Picture SHREK 2

ACCIDENTALLY IN LOVE

E♭ ALTO CLARINET
Band Arrangement

Words and Music by
ADAM F. DURITZ
Arranged by MICHAEL SWEENEY

Moderate Rock

ALSO SPRACH ZARATHUSTRA

Eb ALTO CLARINET
Band Arrangement

By RICHARD STRAUSS
Arranged by MICHAEL SWEENEY

00860144

From the Paramount Motion Picture MISSION: IMPOSSIBLE

MISSION: IMPOSSIBLE THEME

Eb **ALTO CLARINET**
Band Arrangement

By **LALO SCHIFRIN**
Arranged by MICHAEL SWEENEY

Moderately Fast
(3 + 2)

From SHREK
MUSIC FROM SHREK
(A medley including: Fairytale Opening • Ride The Dragon)

E♭ ALTO CLARINET
Band Arrangement

Music by JOHN POWELL and HARRY GREGSON-WILLIAMS
Arranged by JOHN MOSS

00860144

From the TriStar Motion Picture THE MASK OF ZORRO

ZORRO'S THEME

E♭ **ALTO CLARINET**
Band Arrangement

Composed by JAMES HORNER
Arranged by JOHN MOSS

MORE FAVORITES FROM ESSENTIAL ELEMENTS

CHRISTMAS FAVORITES FOR STRINGS
VIOLIN
Solos and String Orchestra Arrangements
Correlated with Essential Elements For Strings

MOVIE FAVORITES FOR STRINGS
VIOLIN
Solos and String Orchestra Arrangements
Correlated with Essential Elements® For Strings
ARRANGED BY ELLIOT DEL BORGO
Includes: Orchestra Arrangement

BROADWAY FAVORITES FOR STRINGS
VIOLIN
Solos and String Orchestra Arrangements
Correlated with Essential Elements® For Strings

PATRIOTIC FAVORITES
VIOLIN
Solos and String Orchestra Arrangements
Correlated with Essential Elements® For Strings
ARRANGED BY JOHN MOSS
Each Song Includes: Solo Page and String Orchestra Arrangement

These superb collections feature favorite songs that students can play as they progress through their string method books. Each song is arranged to be played by either an orchestra or by soloists, with optional accompaniment on CD.

Each song appears twice in the book, featuring:
- Solo instrument version
- String arrangement for orchestra or ensembles
- Accompaniment CD included with conductor's score
- Accompaniment CD available separately
- Piano accompaniment book that is compatible with recorded backgrounds

Available:
- Conductor
- Violin
- Viola
- Cello
- String Bass

- Accompaniment CDs
- Value Starter Pak
  (includes 24 Student books
  plus Conductor Book w/CD

CHRISTMAS FAVORITES
Arranged by Lloyd Conley
Songs include:
The Christmas Song
 (Chestnuts Roasting
 on an Open Fire)
Frosty the Snow Man
A Holly Jolly Christmas
Jingle-Bell Rock
Let It Snow! Let It Snow! Let It Snow!
Rockin' Around the Christmas Tree
We Wish You a Merry Christmas

BROADWAY FAVORITES
Arranged by Lloyd Conley
Songs include:
Beauty and the Beast
Cabaret
Edelweiss
Get Me to the Church on Time
I Dreamed a Dream
Go Go Go Joseph
Memory
The Phantom of the Opera
Seventy Six Trombones

MOVIE FAVORITES
Arranged by Elliot Del Borgo
Includes themes from:
An American Tail
Chariots of Fire
Apollo 13
E.T.
Forrest Gump
Dances with Wolves
Jurassic Park
The Man from Snowy River
Star Trek
Mission: Impossible

PATRIOTIC FAVORITES
Arranged by John Moss
Songs include:
America, the Beautiful
Battle Hymn of the Republic
God Bless America
Hymn to the Fallen
My Country, 'Tis of Thee (America)
The Patriot
The Star Spangled Banner
Stars and Stripes Forever
This Is My Country
Yankee Doodle

FOR MORE INFORMATION, SEE YOUR LOCAL MUSIC DEALER, OR WRITE TO:

HAL•LEONARD®
CORPORATION
7777 W. BLUEMOUND RD. P.O. BOX 13819 MILWAUKEE, WI 53213
Visit Hal Leonard Online at **www.halleonard.com**